The Black Kalendar of Aberdeen

1746 - 1878

Indexed
by
Keith Ferguson

No part of this publication may be reproduced, stored in a retrieval system or transmitted in any form or by any means electronic, mechanical, photocopying, microfilming, recording or otherwise without the prior permission of the Aberdeen and North East Scotland Family History Society.

Copyright (c) Keith Ferguson and Aberdeen and North East Scotland Family History Society.

First published September 1995

ISBN 0-947659-98-6

Published by Aberdeen and North East Scotland Family History Society
164 King Street, Aberdeen AB2 3BD

Printed by
Rainbow Enterprises, Howe Moss Crescent, Kirkhill Industrial Estate, Dyce, Aberdeen

INTRODUCTION

The following pages provide a condensation, in alphabetical order, of "The Black Kalendar of Aberdeen", 4th edition, published in 1878 by James Daniel & Son, Castle Street, Aberdeen. This rare book was loaned to me by an Aberdeen friend who knew I was researching my wife's North-east forebears. Perhaps our friend had doubts about her credentials, but no evidence against her family was found! To make it easier for others I thought I had better index the book.

The Black Kalendar contained "brief accounts of the lives of criminals who may truly be said to be distinguished - not for their good, but for their bad deeds; and though persons who have broken the laws of God and their country yet there were traits in the characters of some of them that showed, had they been trained in the paths of virtue instead of the paths of vice, they would have become distinguished and worthy members of society, instead of outcasts from the community". The period covered is 1746 to 1878.

The purpose of this condensation is to provide a source of reference for those researching their ancestry in the north-east of Scotland. At a distance of several generations, it is acceptable, even exciting, to find one of one's forebears engaged in nefarious activities! Not only criminals are involved of course; the Kalendar mentions many names of witnesses, victims and others.

Where execution was ordered, the Kalendar goes into great detail of the last few days or hours of the condemned person, when every effort was made to extract a confession and bring about a proper state of religious penitence. The actual hangings, generally well attended, are also described in detail.

The numbers after each entry refer to the page numbers in the 4th edition of The Black Kalendar. The spelling of place-names is as given in the Kalendar. Where no other place-name is given, it may be assumed that the case took place in the city of Aberdeen. 'Stouthrief' means 'robbery with violence'; 'sorning' means obtaining free board and lodging by force or threats; the meaning of other Scottish legal terms should be clear from the context.

Keith Ferguson

ACKNOWLEDGEMENT

The Society is grateful to Mr. Ferguson who volunteered to index this work; and to local members for final preparation of the text for publication.

ABERCROMBIE	Robert		Minister of Leslie. House 'completely pillaged' Oct 1746 by outlawed rebels. (1)
ABERNETHY	James		of Mayen. Indicted for murder of John Leith of Leithhall 1764, but believed to have escaped overseas. (60)
ADAM	George		Apprentice, Aberdeen. Procured indenture discharge and promissory note from master, 1791. Imprisoned 3 months, banished 14 years. (140)
ADAMSON	Henry		Ship broker. Witness 1837 in case of Alex Milne v John Anderson & Co (qv). (227)
ADEN	John		Labourer, St Fergus. Witness 1854 in trial of Dr. William Smith (qv). Admonished for prevarication. (270)
AGNEW	Mrs.		Guilty of adultery with Rev. Wm Nesbit (qv). (40)
ALLAN	William		Crofter, parish of Monquhitter. Father from Tarves. Aged 20 when convicted 1825 of murder of Alex Mackay. Married about a year. Hanged. (204)
ALLARDES	William		Stocking Merchant, Aberdeen. Brought charge of assault against Alex Frost (qv), 1777. (95)
AMOS	Flora		Child stolen 1808 by Rachel Wright (qv). (116)
ANDERSON	Alexander		Pled guilty 1849 to culpable homicide of child. Sentenced to 20 years' transportation. (262)
ANDERSON	Alexander		Shoemaker, aged 45. Charged 1858 with incest with 2 daughters. Found guilty and sentenced to penal servitude for life. (289)
ANDERSON	Elizabeth		Aged about 40 in 1821. Murdered by Robert Mackintosh of Crathie (qv). (187)
ANDERSON	John & Co.		Publishers of 'Aberdeen Shaver'. Sued 1837 by Alex Milne (qv) for defamation. (227)
ANDERSON	Patrick		Servant to Alex Nicol, Insch. Murdered, possibly by Donald Fraser (qv), 1749. (52)
ANDERSON	Patrick		Escaped 1787, with Peter Young (qv) while under sentence of transportation. (127)

ANDERSON	William	Farmer, Cairntown of Cowburty. Owner of ox stolen by Alex Martin (qv). (25)
ANNAND	Isobel	Sentenced 1763 to transportation for life for theft. (59)
ANNESLEY	Walter	Soldier in 6th Regt. of Foot. Stole meal from ship at Banff. Sentenced to be whipped and banished to plantations but released by mob, 1766. (66)
ATKINSON	James	Drummer, 6th Regt. of Foot. Found not guilty of theft of meal from ship at Banff, 1766. (66)
BAIGRIE	John	Young seaman, Peterhead. Guilty of assaulting Catherine Davidson, 1858. 8 months' imprisonment. (289)
BAILLIE	James	Condemned to death in Edinburgh 1771 for murder of wife. Pardoned, re-condemned, pardoned again. (98)
BAIN	William	Peterhead. Pled guilty 1855 to culpable homicide of James Grant. 15 years' transportation. (285)
BANNERMAN	Marjory or May	Charged with murder of her child, but plea of concealment of pregnancy accepted, 1849. 12 months' imprisonment. (255)
BARCLAY or GALLOWAY	Jean	Between 60 and 70 in 1857 when murdered by son-in-law John Booth, Oldmeldrum. (285)
BARNETT	Alethia	Wife of Harris Rosenberg, and charged with aiding him in arson at shop in Union Street. 2 years' imprisonment. (235)
BARNETT	John	Marnoch. Servant to John Innes of Muiryfold. Charged with rape of Elizabeth Gills and banished to plantations for life, 1764. (64)
BARNETT or M'BARNETT	John	Kirktown of Peterhead. Theft and housebreaking. Ex-Northern Fencibles and Navy. Hanged 1818. (175)
BARON	Jean	Associate of John Gun (qv), 1754. (38)

BARRON	George		'Country boy', aged 16 in 1819. Grocer's apprentice. Involved by George Watson in false accusation of John Hamilton (qv). (176)
BARRON	Mr.		Druggist in Aberdeen. Witness in case of George Thom (qv), 1821. (179)
BARTLETT	?		Soldier. Shot man in quarrel. Transported. See Peter Young. 1787. (126)
BENZIE	Thomas		'Quackdoctor'. Operated on John Low in Infirmary. Prohibited from 'practising physic and chirurgery' and fined, 1762. (57)
BISSET	Rev. Thomas		Subject of 'theft, fraud and wilful imposition' at hands of Francis Brady and others in train between Stonehaven and Aberdeen, 1859. (290)
BLAIKIE	David		Wright, Hardgate. Murdered 1833 by George Matheson (qv). (221)
BLAIR	John		Soldier in 6th Regiment of Foot. Stole meal from ship at Banff. Sentenced to be whipped and banished to plantations, but released by mob, 1766. (66)
BOOTH	James		Tailor in Banff. Witness in Northfield case. See William Keith. 1766. (68)
BOOTH	John		Hawker, aged 37, Oldmeldrum. Tried 1857 for murder of Jean Barclay (qv). Found guilty and hanged. (285)
BOSS	Corporal		Acted along with William Stables (qv), 1751. (23)
BRADY	Francis		Edinburgh. Charged along with others 1859 with 'theft, fraud and wilful imposition' committed on Rev. Thomas Bisset in train between Stonehaven and Aberdeen. 6 years' penal servitude. (290)
BRAND	Robert		alias 'Coachy' Brand. Coach-wright and builder, Aberdeen. Found not guilty in 1767 of murder of James Murray (qv). (81)
BREBNER	Ann		Died 1785 as result of abortion allegedly procured by Robt Joyner and Robt Dalrymple (qv). (118)

BROWN	?	Glenesk. Murdered by a man Christison (qv) at Stylemouth, 1776. (109)
BROWN	Agnes	From Lochgelly, Fife. Associate of John Gun (qv), also of Peter Young (qv). Charged with pickpocketing 1787 at execution of William Webster. Sentenced to be whipped through the town and banished for 7 years. Married name Graham. (123)
BROWN	Christopher	Labourer, Printfield. Killed 1839 by William M'Donald (qv). (232)
BROWN	Elizabeth	Mother of Agnes Brown (qv). (39)
BROWN	John	See John Munro. (2)
BROWN	Margaret	Mother of Jean Wilson (qv). Sentenced 1776 to 7 years' transportation as May/Maevey alias Macphail alias Margaret Steel. Escaped after 2 years in jail. (127)
BROWNIE	George	Servant to Malcolm Gillespie (qv). Convicted 1827 of fire-raising. 7 years' transportation. (210)
BRUCE	Charles	Outlawed 1849 for non-appearance. (263)
BRUCE	Elspet	Servant. Witness in Northfield case. See William Keith. 1766. (68)
BRUCE	William	Chainmaker, Aberdeen. Tried 1841 for murder of John Williamson. Found guilty of culpable homicide. 12 months' imprisonment. (233)
BUCHAN	Catherine	See Catherine Tawse.
BUCHAN	John	Constable in Stonehaven. Injured 1770 in trying to arrest Thomas Stewart (qv). (87)
BUCHANAN	Henry	Officer of Excise. 1749. Husband of Anne Philp (qv). (15)
BUCHANAN	William	Fifeshire. Ex-compositor in printworks. Once co-tacksman of quarry near Peterhead. Convicted 1823 of 'stouthrief' committed on John Cooper. Hanged. (193)
BUCK	Alex Jnr.	Laxfisher, Banchory. Outlawed 1760 for non-appearance on charge of murder. (55)

BURNETT	Charles	Wright in Stonehaven. Killed in affray in public-house at Cairnhill on Stonehaven Road, when Lieut. Farquharson also injured, 1769. See James Williamson. (85)
BURNETT	George	Convicted 1749 of horse-stealing. Escaped along with Alex Macdonald (qv), outlawed, recaptured, banished for life. (17)
BURNETT	James	Farm servant, Protshaugh, Tyrie. Aged 44 when convicted 1849 of murder of wife Margaret Murray. Hanged. (248)
BURNETT	William	of Strachan. Hanged 1783 for theft of mare and ox. (112)
BURR	Alexander	Charged 1815 with rioting etc. at house of Margaret Dick (qv). Not proven. (168)
BYRES	Patrick	of Tonley. Believed to have abetted and escaped with James Abernethy (qv), 1763. (60)
CAMERON	Angus	Witness in case of murder of Sergeant Davis (qv), 1754. (41)
CAMERON	William	See Hugh Thompson.
CAMPBELL	Alexandrina	Servant to Malcolm Gillespie (qv). Convicted 1827 of fire-raising. 7 years' transportation. (210)
CARLE	James	Weaver. Tried 1800 for murder of Margaret Keith at Auchtydonald, Banffshire. Not proven. (148)
CARTY	Jean	Aged 24 or 25 in 1849. Servant at Protshaugh, Tyrie. Paramour and witness in case of James Burnett (qv). (248)
CHALMERS	John	Charged along with William Wilson (qv) but libel found not proven. (8)
CHANNON	Thomas	Soldier in General Wolfe's Regiment. Engaged by Synod of Aberdeen to improve religious singing. Aroused ire of Gideon Duncan (qv). (28)
CHAPMAN	James	Hangman or 'dempster' at execution of Alexander Cheyne (qv). (6)

CHEYNE	Alexander		Mill of Macterry in the parish of Fyvie. Theft, housebreaking, burning and torturing. Executed 8 September 1748. (6)
CHRISTIE	Alexander		Howmills, Glass. Adultery and incest with Janet Smith, natural daughter of wife Isobel Macdonald. Banished for life to plantations, 1776. (106)
CHRISTIE	George		Lower Denburn, Aberdeen. Native of Skene. Ex-East India Co. Earlier stole silver plate from Murtle House. Convicted and hanged 1852 for murder of Barbara Ross and grandson at Sunnybank near Kittybrewster Toll-bar. (264)
CHRISTISON	?		Glenesk. Murdered a man Brown 1776 at Stylemouth. Outlawed. (109)
CHRISTISON	Agnes		Associate of James Davidson (qv). (2)
CLARK	Ann		Sister of Christian Clark (qv). Indicted for similar offences but fled. (52)
CLARK	Christian		Banished the county for 'entertaining men... and sailors upon Sundays' etc, 1756. (52)
CLARK	Elizabeth		Aged 13 in 1849 when witness in case of murder of mother by William Clark (qv). (259)
CLARK	John		Woolcomber, Aberdeen. Convicted 1772 of conspiring to murder Alexander Frost. Banished to plantations 10 years. (95)
CLARK	William		Tinker, aged 40. Charged 1849 with murder of wife Bridget Conlie or Connolly, on the Esslemont Road near Ellon. Not proven. (259)
CLARK	William		Edinburgh. Charged along with others 1859 with 'theft, fraud and wilful imposition' committed on Rev. Thomas Bisset in train between Stonehaven and Aberdeen. Did not appear; sentence of fugitation. (290)

CLERK or TERIG	Duncan	Glenaye. Charged along with Alex Bane Macdonald with murder of Sergeant Arthur Davis of General Guise's Regt., 1749. Found not guilty, 1754. (41)
COLKAT	Elizabeth	Wife of James Davidson (qv). (2)
COLLIE	James	Horsehirer at Gallowgate. Convicted of assault on woman with intent to ravish. Whipped through the streets and banished to the plantations for life, 1763. (59)
CONLIE or CONNOLLY	Bridget	Allegedly murdered 1849 by husband William Clerk and Janet Gray or Thomson (qv). (259)
COOPER	John	Farmer, Newton-of-Greens, Monquhitter. Subject of 'stouthrief' 1823 at hands of Thomas Donaldson, William Buchanan and William Forbes Duncan (qv). (193)
COURT	Samuel	Soldier in General Campbell's Regt. Indicted 1756 'for a capital offence', but found not proven. (58)
CRAIG	Mrs.	Widow aged 59. 7½ Canal Street, Aberdeen. Murdered 1867. See John Craig. (304)
CRAIG	Jean	Huntly. Various theft charges. Successively sentenced to be whipped, banished, executed. Hanged 1784. (111)
CRAIG	John	One of sons of Mrs. Craig, 7½ Canal Street, Aberdeen. Charged 1867 with her murder. Found not proven. Brother David a sea-captain. (308)
CREEK	Margaret	Kept house of ill-fame near Justice-Port where John Simpson (qv) murdered, 1807. Witness. (162)
CRUICKSHANK	Jane	Aberchirder. Sentenced 1860 to 9 months' imprisonment for concealment of pregnancy. (293)
CULLEN	James Jnr.	Mosstown of Crimond. Found not guilty of rape of and incest with stepmother, 1768. (83)
CUMMINE	John	See John M'Gibbon.

CUMMING	James		Charged 1855 with theft of or fraudulently obtaining horse. Guilty. 7 years' transportation. (256)
DALRYMPLE	Robert		Flaxdresser, Aberdeen. Charged along with Robert Joyner 1785 with procuring abortion on Ann Brebner and Martha Stewart, who died. Found not proven. (118)
DAVIDSON	Barbara		Kincardineshire. Guilty 1772 of child murder. Death sentence commuted to banishment to plantations for life. (96)
DAVIDSON	Catherine		Wife of James Humphrey. Convicted 1830 of his murder and hanged. (215)
DAVIDSON	Catherine		Tillyfro Cottage. Allegedly murdered 1855 by William Davidson (qv). (282)
DAVIDSON	Catherine		Backgate Street, Peterhead. Assaulted by John Baigrie (qv), 1858. (289)
DAVIDSON	Donald		'Highlander'. Railway navvy. Convicted 1848 of being part of riotous mob in Stonehaven when William Murray was killed. 7 years' transportation. (245)
DAVIDSON	James		Jacobite, army deserter, native of Brechin. Committed numerous 'sornings', house-breaking and robberies, specialising in manses, 1747-48. Executed 1 July 1748. (2)
DAVIDSON	James		See Hugh Graham.
DAVIDSON	John		Miller at Gordon's Mills. Charged with assaulting wife and daughter-in-law, 1765. Guilty of former. Whipped through the streets and banished for 7 years. (65)
DAVIDSON	John (2)		Waterside of Ythan. Deponed that he was 'in dread of bodily harm' from Wm. Philp (qv), 1769. (84)
DAVIDSON	John (3)		Salmon fisher, Bridge of Don. Along with William Henderson, charged 1783 with 'battery and bloodwit' on William Davidson. Fined £5 to pursuers and £5 to procurator-fiscal. (113)
DAVIDSON	Margaret		Daughter of John Davidson (qv). (65)

DAVIDSON	Mary	A 'caird', associate of John Gun (qv). Died in prison, 1765. (37 and 65)
DAVIDSON	William	Vintner in Old Aberdeen. Assaulted 1782 by John Davidson (3) and William Henderson (qv). (113)
DAVIDSON	William	Tillyfro Cottage. Tried 1855 for murder of Catherine Davidson. Not proven. (282)
DAVIS	Sgt. William	General Guise's Regt. Victim of murder for which Duncan Clerk and Alex Bane (qv) charged. (41)
DAWSON	Charles	Town-sergeant 1842. (236)
DEWAR	Very Rev.	Principal and Mrs. Albyn Place. See Christian King. (223)
DICK	Margaret	(Meggie Dickie) alias Hall. Kept disreputable house, 'the White Ship', 'between the hills' in Aberdeen. Subject of a riot in 1815. (168)
DICKIE	Henry D	Manager, Caledonian Insce Co., Edinburgh. Witness 1854 in trial of Dr. William Smith (qv). (270)
DINGWALL	(Captain) Alexander	Ex-sailing master on East India Co. vessels. Stonehaven. Charged 1867 with murder of wife. Found guilty of culpable homicide and sentenced to 10 years' penal servitude. (299)
DONALD	Andrew	Weaver in Aberdeen. Convicted 1817 of shopbreaking. Transported for life. (171)
DONALD	John	See John M'Donald.
DONALD	W	Union Whale Fishery Co. Witness 1837 in case of Alex Milne (qv). (227)
DONALDSON	Thomas	Parish of Ellon. Once tacksman of quarry near Peterhead. Convicted 1823 of 'stouthrief' committed on John Cooper. Hanged. (193)
DOUGHERTY	Hugh	Edinburgh. Charged along with others 1859 with 'theft, fraud and wilful imposition' committed on Rev. Thomas Bisset in train between Stonehaven and Aberdeen. 6 years' penal servitude. (290)

DOUGLAS	Janet	Sentenced to death 1817 for child stealing, but sentence commuted. (118)
DOUGLAS	John	Charged 1815 with rioting etc. at house of Margaret Dick (qv). 7 years' transportation. (168)
DOW	Rev.	Minister of Fettercairn. Attacked by James Davidson (qv) whom he kept prisoner for a time. (2)
DOWNIE	James	Factor to Haughton. Allegedly murdered by Charles Sievewright, 1768. (84)
DUN	Jean	Daughter-in-law of John Davidson (qv). (65)
DUN	John	Associate of James Davidson (qv). (2)
DUN	Mary	Wife of John Davidson (qv). (65)
DUNCAN	Bethridge	Lumsden. Sentenced 1860 to 9 months' imprisonment for concealment of pregnancy. (292)
DUNCAN	Gideon	Weaver, Old Aberdeen. Charged with 'disturbing congregation' by deliberately singing out of tune etc. Fined £50 Scots, 1753. (28)
DUNCAN	James	Whitefield. Witness in Northfield case, 1766. (68)
DUNCAN	James	Aged 18. Son of stocking-dresser in Aberdeen. Career of theft and housebreaking. Banished overseas, 1771. (88)
DUNCAN	James	See James Watt.
DUNCAN	William Forbes	Pled guilty to theft and 'stouthrief' on John Cooper, 1823. Transported for life. (193)
DUTCH	John	Servant to George Burnet, Esq of Kemnay. Outlawed for non-appearance on charge of murder, 1764. (60)
EDGAR	John	Soldier in Lord Hopetoun's Fencibles. Charged with aiding and abetting Wm. Turnbull (qv), 1794, but pardoned on condition entered King's service. (142)
EDWARDS	George Skene	Clerk to Malcolm Gillespie (qv). Convicted 1827 of forgery. Banished for life. (210)

EDWARDS	James		Woolcomber, Aberdeen. Not proven, 1772, on charge of conspiring to murder Alexander Frost (qv). (95)
EDWARDS	John		Brother of George (qv). (210)
ELDER	Margaret		Huntly(?). Associate of Jean Craig (qv). Sentenced to death 1783 for housebreaking and theft, but this commuted to banishment for life. (111)
ELLIS	Alex		Sergeant, 6th Regt. of Foot. Not guilty of theft of meal from ship at Banff, 1766. (66)
ESSON	James		Parish of Logie Coldstone. Charged 1815 with murder of mother, but unfit to stand trial because of 'general idiocy'. (168)
ESSON	Robert		Murdered at Woolmanhill 1749 by A. Philp and A. Macdonald (qv). (16)
FALCONER	Mrs.		Wife of David. Sister-in-law of Thomas Fyfe (qv), witness in Captain Dingwall case. (299)
FARQUHARSON	Alex		Inverey. Juryman in Northfield case, 1766. (68)
FARQUHARSON	(Lieut.) Charles		of Coldrach. Injured in affray in public-house at Cairnhill on Stonehaven Road in incident when Charles Burnett died, 1769. Cleared of assault. See James Williamson. (85)
FARQUHARSON	Donald		Glendee. Witness in case of Sergeant Davis (qv). (41)
FARQUHARSON	Findlay		'Young lad'. Murdered 1800 in Skellater House, home of Mr. Forbes. Murderer Paul Michie escaped and outlawed. (149)
FARQUHARSON	Francis		Finzean. Juryman in Northfield case, 1766. (68)
FERGUSON	Rev.		Minister of Farnell. Robbed of £10 and watch by James Davidson (qv), 1748. (2)
FISHER	Basil		Lessee of Thainston House and shootings. Mentioned in 1864 murder of Ann Forbes (qv). (295)

FORBES	Ann	Wife of William Forbes, Shoemaker, Virginia Street, Aberdeen. Murdered 1864 by George Stephen (qv) in woods of Thainston, aged 52 or 53. (295)
FORBES	Francis	East Middleton, Banchory-Devenick. Aged 27 when tried 1854 for murder of Ann Harvey (qv) at Cults. Not proven. (279)
FORBES	John	Invernan. Juryman in Northfield case, 1766. (68)
FORBES	Margaret	Banished 1755/6 for child-murder. (52)
FORBES	Theodore	Mill-of-Pettie. Outlawed 1760 for non-appearance on charge of murder. (55)
FORBES	William	Skellater. Juryman in Northfield case, 1766. (68)
FORDYCE	John	Ardoe. Juryman in Northfield case, 1766. (68)
FORDYCE	John	Blacksmith at Howburn (Holburn). Tried 1804 for murder of wife Jean Mackenzie. Found guilty of culpable homicide. 6 months' imprisonment and banished Scotland 14 years. (161)
FOREMAN	Alex	Farmer, Kirktown, St. Fergus. Witness 1854 in trial of Dr. William Smith (qv). (270)
FORSYTH	Alex	Not guilty of theft of meal from ship at Banff, 1766. (66)
FORSYTH	James	'County policeman' who arrested James Burnett (qv), 1849. (248)
FOSTER	Joseph	Wright, Aberdeen. Juryman in Northfield case, 1766. (68)
FRAIN	Adam	Apprentice to James Dyce, barber in Aberdeen. Convicted of housebreaking. Sentenced 1771 to be publicly whipped and banished the county. (91)
FRASER	Alexander	Sentenced 1849 to 7 years' transportation for pickpocketing. (263)
FRASER	Andrew	See Andrew Hosack.

FRASER	Donald		Soldier, Cameronian Regt. Charged 1757 with murder of Patrick Anderson, Insch in 1749. Trial thought to have failed for lack of evidence. (52)
FRASER	Kenneth		Witness at trial of Hugh M'Leod for murder of Murdo Grant, Inverness, 1831. (46)
FRASER	William		The bellman, St. Fergus. Witness 1854 in trial of Dr. William Smith (qv). (270)
FROST	Alexander		Woolcomber, Aberdeen. Broke away from league of colleagues who conspired to murder him, 1769. See also William Allardes. (94)
FULLERTON	Mr.		of Dudwick. House broken into by John Hutcheon (qv), 1763. (64)
FYFE	Thomas		Landlord of Captain and Mrs Alex Dingwall (qv) and witness in case against Capt Dingwall for murder of his wife, 1867. (299)
GALLOWAY	Jean		See Jean Barclay.
GATHERER	Ann		See Ann Geddes.
GEDDES	Alexander		Kinnermony, Banffshire. In 1751, the last person to be executed by burning in Aberdeen. (22)
GEDDES or GATHERER	Ann		Found guilty 1849 of pickpocketing and sentenced to 7 years' transportation. (263)
GERRIE	Peter Coutts		General Merchant, Torphins. Shot at by William M'Petrie (qv), 1878, and wounded. (311)
GIBB	William		'Boy'. Killed in Ross & Cromarty Rangers riot, 1802. (153)
GIBBONS	John		Chelsea Pensioner. Convicted 1772 of conspiring to murder Alexander Frost. (95)
GIBSON	Daniel		A 'boy' in 1849 when sentenced to 10 years' transportation for theft. (262)
GILL	Helen		Tried 1849 for theft. Sentenced to 7 years' transportation. (255)
GILL	Thomas		Allegedly murdered in 1817 by George Thom (qv). (186)

GILLESPIE	Alex	Slater, Tough. Murdered 1790 by James Henderson (qv) at Forgue. (136)
GILLESPIE	Malcolm	Excise Officer, Crombie Cottage. Convicted 1827 of forgery and 'uttering'. Hanged. (210)
GLASS	James	See James Grant.
GLEN	Alex	See John M'Donald.
GLENNIE	Alexander	Charged 1864 with 12 acts of theft by housebreaking from premises in Exchange Court, Union Street and Crown Court. Found guilty of theft and sentenced to 8 years' penal servitude. (293)
GODSMAN	Helen	Fyvie. Suspected of child murder but not brought to trial. 1771. (90)
GORDON	George	Professor of Oriental Languages at King's College. Bailie who convicted Gideon Duncan (qv), 1753. (28)
GORDON	Helen	Witness 1821 in case of Robert Mackintosh (qv). (187)
GORDON	James	Techmuiry. Witness in Northfield case, 1766. (68)
GORDON	John	Garbelly, Dundurcus. Convicted 1767 of horse-stealing. Sentenced to death but pardoned on condition left country. Either did not, or returned, as original sentence revived, though believed to have died in prison 1773. (97)
GORDON	Patrick	From Braemar. Banished 1751 for being a Catholic Priest. (21)
GORDON	William	Aberdeen. Sentenced to death 1821 for murder of wife. Tried escape with Robert Mackintosh. (189)
GOW	William	Auchenrach, Cabrach. Shot 1751 by Thomas Stables (qv). (23)
GRAHAM	Hugh	alias James Davidson. Died in fight with John Young (qv), 1801. (150)
GRAHAM	James	Soldier. Charged 1807 with murder of John Simpson (qv). (162)

GRANT	Alexandrina	alias Jemima McKenzie. Transported for 7 years for fraud on Mrs. Lindsay, Huntly Street and Mrs. McDonald, High Street, 1844. (240)
GRANT	Charles	Inveravon. Roman Catholic. Guilty of fire-raising etc. and hanged 26 January 1750. (18)
GRANT	Elspet	Convicted 1751 of sheep-stealing along with husband William Macdonald. (25)
GRANT	James	Tinsmith, Peterhead. Killed in 1855 by William Bain (qv). (285)
GRANT	James	alias Glass. Guilty 1788 of shopbreaking and theft. Hanged. (134)
GRANT	James	Kincardineshire. Arrested for sheep-stealing. Died at Bridge of Dee trying to escape, 1811 or 1818. (174)
GRANT	John	See Malcolm Macgregor.
GRANT	John	Son of James Grant, Richaillagh, Strathspey. Murdered 1772 by John M'Gibbon (qv). (96)
GRANT	Murdo	Murder victim of Hugh M'Leod (qv), 1831. (46)
GRANT	William	Convicted 1750 for being 'habit and repute a Priest, Jesuit or trafficking Papist'. Banished. (20)
GRANT	William	Witness 1832 to assault on Francis Middleton by John Stewart. (229)
GRAY	Adam	Brother of Provost of Peterhead. Witness 1854 in trial of Dr. William Smith (qv). (270)
GRAY	Agnes	Associate of James Stewart (qv). Banished country, 1790. (135)
GRAY	Andrew	Jailer at Aberdeen at time of escape of Peter Young (qv), 1787. Dismissed for negligence. (124)
GRAY	James	Son of John Gray, Pitmedden. Charged 1770 along with Christian Spence for fire-raising. Banished Scotland for life. (88)
GRAY	Janet	See Janet Thomson.

GRAY	Sophia		Associate of James Stewart (qv). Banished country, 1790. (135)
GRAY	William		Merchant. 'Elected' jailer at Aberdeen 1754, replacing Alex Thomson. (51)
GREEN	George		Edinburgh. Charged along with others 1859 with 'theft, fraud and wilful imposition' committed on Rev. Thomas Bisset in train between Stonehaven and Aberdeen. 7 years' penal servitude. (290)
GREIG	Jessie		Housekeeper to Malcolm Gillespie (qv), 1827. (210)
GREWAR	John		Inverey. Witness in case of murder of Sergeant Davis, 1754. (41)
GRIERSON	Malcolm		See Malcolm Macgregor.
GUN(N)	John		Noted Highland robber in style of Rob Roy. Sentenced to death for theft but reprieved and banished to Virginia with wife and daughter Sarah, 1754. (36)
HALL	Margaret		See Margaret Dick.
HAMILTON	John		Cutler, Gallowgate. Falsely accused of housebreaking by George Watson (qv), 1819. (176)
HARPER	Mr.		Schoolmaster of Durris. Robbed of £35 by James Davidson (qv), 1748. (2)
HARROW	John		Barber. Convicted 1758 of trying to strangle apprentice James Legge. Fined and excluded from Trades' Corporation. (54)
HARVEY	Ann		'Young woman' employed at Peterculter paper mills. Allegedly murdered by Frances Forbes, 1854. (279)
HENDERSON	James		Bainshole, Forgue. Along with wife Eliz. Stewart charged 1790 with murder of Alex Gillespie. Found guilty and hanged. (136)
HENDERSON	William		Salmon fisher, Old Aberdeen. Along with John Davidson charged 1783 with 'battery and bloodwit' on William Davidson. Fined £5 to pursuers and £5 to procurator-fiscal. (113)

HERVIE	Alexander	Kemnay. Aged 80 in 1824 when subject of 'stouthrief' at hands of Alex Martin (qv). (198)
HERVIE	Christian	Daughter of Alexander. Subject of 'stouthrief' 1824 at hands of Alex Martin (qv). (198)
HOSACK	Andrew	alias Fraser. Convicted 1810 of housebreaking at Rubislaw. While lying under sentence of death, came under suspicion of murdering George and Margaret Milne. Denied it. Hanged. Catholic. (165)
HOSACK or HOSIE	William	Woolcomber, Aberdeen. Convicted 1772 of conspiring to murder Alexander Frost. Banished to plantations for 10 years. (95)
HUMPHREY	James	Butcher. Also kept public house in 'low quarter of the town'. Murdered by wife Catherine Davidson (qv), 1830. (215)
HUTCHEON	Alexander	Nigg. Charged with rape, 1754. (51)
HUTCHEON	Arthur	Parish of Old Deer. Brother and suspected accomplice of John Hutcheon (qv), 1765. (64)
HUTCHEON	John	Farmer at Carnabog of Carnousie, previously Ardargue in Dudwick. Housebreaking and theft. Hanged 1765. (64).
HUTCHISON	James	Auctioneer, Peterhead. Witness 1854 in trial of Dr. William Smith (qv). (270)
IMLACH	Elspet	Murdered 1800 allegedly by William Morrison (qv). (145)
INGLIS	Anne	Charged 1795 with murder by poison of Patrick Pirie, Malhereust, Alva, to whom she had been servant. Found not guilty. (142)
INGRAM	George	Piper. Murdered at a 'penny wedding' near Ellon, 1754. (51)
INNES	George	Aged 13 in 1838 when witness to assault on Francis Middleton by John Stewart. (229)
INNES	Lewis	Balnacraig. Juryman in Northfield case, 1766. (68)
IRVINE	Dr.	Witness in Northfield case, 1766. (68)

IRVINE	Alexander	Shoemaker, Echt. Charged 1754 with rape of Isobel Wright. Escaped and outlawed but later recaptured and sent to the fleet. (51)
IRVINE	Margaret	Native of Orkney. Servant to Alex Pride, tailor, Edinburgh. Charged 1784 with man-stealing (plagium) of George, child of latter, taking him to Aberdeen and using him for begging. Transported for life. (115)
JACKSON	Thomas	Pled guilty 1849 to theft by housebreaking. 10 years' transportation. (255)
JAMIESON	Margaret	Aged 13 when raped 1849 by Alex Mackie (qv) in quarry between Bridge of Don and Grandholme. (263)
JENKINS	William	Servant to Malcolm Gillespie (qv), 1827. (210)
JOHNSTON	Arthur	Lieut. and Adjutant of St George's Dragoons at execution of James Davidson (qv), 1748. (2)
JOHNSTONE	Ninian	Merchant, Aberdeen. Juryman in Northfield case, 1766. (68)
JOYNER	Robert	Druggist, Aberdeen. Along with Robert Dalrymple, charged 1785 with procuring abortion on Ann Brebner and Martha Stewart, who died. Fled and outlawed. (118)
JOYNER	William	Servant to Donald Mackenzie, horse-hirer in Aberdeen. Convicted 1765 of theft of mail at Bervie. Banished for life. (58)
KEITH	Dr.	Witness 1833 in case of Christian King (qv). (223)
KEITH	Alexander	of Northfield, parish of Gamrie. Allegedly murdered 1756 by wife Helen Watt and son William (qv). (68)
KEITH	George	Son of Alexander Keith of Northfield. Secured prosecution of Helen Watt and William Keith for murder of his father. (68)
KEITH	Margaret	Widow. Murdered 1800 allegedly by James Carle. (148)

KEITH	William	Charged 1766 along with mother Helen Watt with murder of father Alexander Keith at Northfield in 1756. Condemned to death but later pardoned. (68)
KENNEDY	John Breck	Convicted for cattle-stealing, 1753. Assaulted hangman. Uncle of John M'Connachy (qv). (8)
KILLHOWLIE	Thomas	Sentenced 1849 to 7 years' transportation for pickpocketing. (263)
KING	Christian	Servant to Very Rev. Principal Dewar of Marischal College, Albyn Place. Convicted 1833 of murder of her infant. Transported for life. (223)
KING	Helen	Charged with adultery with John Taylor, whitefisher of Stonehaven, 1753. (39)
KING	William	Found guilty of theft 1849 and sentenced to 7 years' transportation. (256)
KNOX	Mr.	of Kinnaird. Robbed of silver and other articles to the value of £15 by James Davidson (qv). (2)
KYNOCH	James	'Countryman'. Helped to apprehend James Davidson (qv). (2)
LANGIBEER	Mary Agnes	alias M'Laurin. 'Genteel looking woman'. Fraudulently obtained 111 articles from merchants in city. 12 months' imprisonment. (291)
LANIGAN	Ensign	Ross and Cromarty Rangers. Involved in riot 1802. (153)
LAWSON	Mary	Found guilty 1766 of child-murder and banished for life. Pled unsuccessfully that a man Reid had raped her. (66)
LEASK	Ursula	Servant to Rev. James Robertson, St. Fergus, 1853. See trial of Dr. William Smith. (270)
LEGGE	James	Apprentice to John Harrow, barber, who tried to strangle him, 1758. (54)

LEITH	John		of Leithhall. Died after quarrel with James Abernethy (qv) of Mayen. Widow, Mrs. Harriet Stuart, Lady Leithhall, and sons John, Alexander and James, raised action of assythement but awarded only £200. 1764. (60)
LEITH	William		Froghall. Poultry stolen 1782 by Jean Craig (qv). (110)
LESSEL	George		Pitmedden. Christian Spence and James Gray (qv) set fire to his cotton-yarn, 1770. (88)
LINDSAY	Mrs		Lodging-house keeper, Huntly Street, Aberdeen. Witness in case of Alexandrina Grant (qv), 1844. (240)
LINDSAY	Benjamin		Woolcomber, Aberdeen. Convicted 1772 of conspiring to murder Alexander Frost. Banished for 10 years to plantations. (95)
LITTLEJOHN	John		Woolcomber, Aberdeen. Not proven on charge of conspiring to murder Alexander Frost, 1772. (95)
LIVINGSTONE	Alexander		of Countesswells. Ex-Provost of Aberdeen. In 1753, raised action of criminal slander against James Smith (qv) who alleged he had been responsible for rise in cost of meal. (33)
LORIMER	Alexander		Piper. Charged 1756 with murder of George Ingram (qv) but charge not proceeded with. (51)
LOVIE	John		Farmer, Futteretden, near Fraserburgh. Charged 1827 with murder of Margaret MacKessar. Not proven. (207)
LOW	James		Fiddler, Ellon. Charged 1756 but released along with Alex Lorimer (qv). (51)
LOW	John		Fetteresso. Cancer of lip. Operated on by 'Dr.' Thomas Benzie (qv). (58)
M'BARNETT	John		see John Barnett.
MACALLUM	Donald		Soldier. Charged with murder of John Simpson (qv), 1807. Not proven. (162)

M'CONNACHIE	James		Postrunner. Robbed 1866 while carrying mailbag between Tarland and Aboyne. George Milne (qv) later charged with theft. (298)
M'CONNACHY	John		Convicted for sheep-stealing at Inverness, 1753. Struck hangman at execution. (7)
MACONOCHIE	David		Associate of James Davidson (qv). (2)
M'CRAW	John		Banished 1819 for housebreaking and theft. Would have escaped but for George Watson (qv). (178)
MACDONALD	Alexander		Butcher. Charged along with Alex Philp with murder of Robert Esson at Woolmanhill. Found guilty. Sentenced to death but escaped, 1749. (16)
M'DONALD	Alexander		Found guilty of 'sorning' getting free board and lodgings by force or threats, and banished from the city for life, 1789. (4)
MACDONALD	Alexander Bane		Culloch of Invercauld. Charged along with Duncan Clerk with murder of Sergeant William Davis of General Guise's Regt., 1749. Found not guilty, 1756. (41)
MACDONALD	Elizabeth		See Eliz. Slessor.
MACDONALD	Isobel		Wife of Alex Christie and mother of Janet Smith (qv), Glass, 1776. (106)
M'DONALD	John (1)		Vagrant. Charged 1785 with fire-raising. Hanged. (119)
MACDONALD	John (2)		Witness 1821 in case of Robert Mackintosh (qv). (187)
MACDONALD	William		Convicted 1751 of sheep-stealing along with wife Elspet Grant. (25)
M'DONALD	William		Farmer, Burnside near St. Fergus. Allegedly murdered 1853 by Dr. William Smith (qv). (270)
M'DONALD	William		Night Watchman. Convicted 1839 of culpable homicide of Christopher Brown in West North Street. Transported for life. (232)

MACDONOGH	Capt. Felix Bryan	Ross & Cromarty Rangers. Charged with murder of John Ross in 1802 riot, but found not guilty. (153)
M'FIE	Neil	Banished at Inverness for life 1759 for being 'habit and repute a Popish Priest'. Last case of its kind in Scotland. (21)
MACGHEE	John	Vintner. Fined £5 in 1765 for 'inhospitality' - failing to give lodging to strangers. (67)
McGIBBON or CUMMINE	John	Murdered John Grant 1772 in Strathspey but escaped. (96)
MACGILIES	Alexander	Alias Alexander MACPHERSON (qv). (41)
MACGREGOR	Malcolm or Callum	alias Grierson alias John Grant, Ballymoinde, Glengairne. Charged 1773 with murder of John Stewart, Abergairn, in 1747. Pled that crime had prescribed by lapse of more than 20 years. Discharged. (100)
M'GUIRE	Thomas	Edinburgh. Charged along with others 1859 with 'theft, fraud and wilful imposition' committed on Rev. Thomas Bisset in train between Stonehaven and Aberdeen. 6 years' penal servitude. (290)
MACHARDIE	Isobel	Inverey. Witness in case of murder of Sergeant Davis (qv), 1754. (41)
MACKAY	Alexander	Cattle drover, Sutherlandshire. 'Old man' when murdered 1825 near Fyvie by William Allan. Died despite 'operation of the trepan'. (204)
MACKAY	(Sgt.) Andrew	Ross & Cromarty Rangers. Charged with murder of John Ross in 1802 riot. Not proven. (153)
MACKAY	Donald	Charged 1815 with rioting etc. at house of Margaret Dick (qv). 12 months' confinement at Bridewell. (168)
MACKENZIE	Donald	Horse-hirer in Aberdeen. Employer of William Joyner (qv), 1765. (58)
MACKENZIE	(Col.) George	Ross & Cromarty Rangers. Charged with murder of John Ross in 1802 riot. Not guilty. (153)

MACKENZIE	Jean	Killed by husband John Fordyce (qv), 1804. (161)
McKENZIE	Jemima	See Alexandrina Grant.
MACKENZIE	Kenneth	Merchant, Aberdeen. Juror in Northfield case, 1766. (68)
MACKENZIE	Robert	'Young man'. Married with 2 children. Contractor for excavation and roadmaking, Aberdeen. Sentenced 1878 to 18 months' imprisonment for forging cheques in name of James Ro(d)ger. (313)
MACKESSAR	Margaret	Servant at Futteretden, near Fraserburgh. Allegedly murdered 1827 by John Lovie (qv). (207)
MACKIE	Alexander	Farm Servant. Found guilty 1849 of rape of Margaret Jamieson in quarry between Bridge of Don and Grandholme. Transportation for life. (263)
MACKINTOSH	Robert	Aged 21 in 1821. Farm servant, Crathie. Hanged for murder of Eliz. Anderson though tried to escape along with William Gordon (qv). (187)
M'KRAW	Alexander	See John M'Donald (39).
M'LAURIN	Mary Agnes	See Mary Agnes Langibeer.
M'LEOD	Alexander	Merchant, St. Fergus. Witness 1854 in trial of Dr. William Smith (qv). (270)
M'LEOD	Hugh	Convicted at Inverness of murder of Murdo Grant, 1831. (46)
MACLEOD	Neil	Brother of William. Pled guilty 1823 to 'stouthrief' on Margaret Murray. Transported for life. (195)
MACLEOD	Robert	Aged 36 at time of execution in 1824 for murder of common law wife near summit at Lochmaven. Roman Catholic. (201)
MACLEOD	William	Brother of Neil. Convicted of 'stouthrief' on Margaret Murray, and hanged, 1823. (195)

M'MAHON	Robert		Edinburgh. Charged along with others 1859 with 'theft, fraud and wilful imposition' committed on Rev. Thomas Bisset in train between Stonehaven and Aberdeen. 6 years' penal servitude. (290)
MACMILLAN	John		Jacobite and thief. Executed Inverness, 1755. (5)
M'PETRIE	William		Torphins. Aged 32. Guilty of shooting at and wounding Peter Coutts Gerrie, general merchant, Torphins, 1878. 20 years' penal servitude. (311)
MACPHERSON	Alexander		alias Macgillies. Inverey. Witness in case of Sergeant Davis (qv). (41)
MACPHERSON	Daniel		Soldier. Charged with murder of John Simpson (qv), 1807. Not proven. (162)
M'ROBBIE	Mr.		Gardener at Sunnybank near Kittybrewster Toll-bar in 1852, and witness to murder by George Christie (qv). (264)
MAITLAND	Mr.		Candlemaker. Witness 1837 in case of Alexander Milne (qv). (227)
MAITLAND	Arthur		Pitrichie. Juror in Northfield case, 1766. (68)
MAN	William		Woolcomber, Aberdeen. Convicted 1772 of conspiring to murder Alexander Frost. Banished for life. (95)
MANSON	James		Barber. Witness in Northfield case, 1766. (68)
MARSHALL	Helen		See Helen Whitecross.
MARTIN	Alexander		Tenant in Westertown of Huntly. Convicted of stealing and slaughtering an ox, 1753. (25)
MARTIN	Alexander		Durris. Found not guilty 1823 of rape in 1816 of Christian Moir. Guilty 1824 of 'stouthrief' on Hervie household. Hanged. (198)
MARTIN	James		See William Martin (2). James failed to appear for trial and outlawed. (19)

MARTIN	William (1)	Clockmaker in Old Aberdeen. Had member of company arrested for disrespectful remarks on Royal Family, 1749. (5)
MARTIN	William (2)	Convicted 1749 along with brother James of stealing poor's box from Church of Old Machar. Because of his youth, sentence of death commuted to transportation to West Indies. (19)
MASON	George	Smiddycroft near Jellybrands. Robbed of £40, 1770, by James Duncan (qv). (88)
MATHESON	George	Shoemaker, Holburn Street. Aged 27 in 1833 when convicted of murder of David Blaikie. Transported for life. (221)
MEAD	John	Englishman. Woolcomber, Aberdeen. Assaulted by colleagues for breaching compact, 1769. (93)
MELLIS	James	Town Sergeant, 1842. (236)
MELVIL	Robert	Minister of Durris. Lost 'all his valuables' to James Davidson (qv), 1747. Wife died of shock. (2)
MEYERS	Lazarus	Belgian, in business in Aberdeen for some years. Witness 1848 in case of Eliz. Milne (qv). (246)
MICHIE	Paul	Corryhowl of Corgarff. Catholic. Said to have murdered Findlay Farquharson in Skellater House. Outlawed, 1801. (149)
MIDDLETON	Francis	Tenant farmer, Shank, Aberdour. Murdered 1838 by John Stewart (qv). (229)
MILLER	James	Whipped through streets for theft, and ordered to be banished. Then convicted for housebreaking at Inverurie and hanged, 1753. (35)
MILNE	Alexander	Lime and coal merchant. Sued publishers of 'Aberdeen Shaver' in 1837 for defamation and awarded £150. (227)
MILNE	Elizabeth	Aged 15 when convicted 1848 of theft from Lazarus Meyers (qv). 15 months' imprisonment. (246)

MILNE	George	Constable at Tarland. Charged 1866 with theft from James M'Connachie (qv). Found not proven. Money returned a few days after trial. (298)
MILNE	George	Cottertown of Auchanasie, near Keith. Aged over 80 when murdered 1797. Murder later attributed to but denied by Andrew Hosack (qv). (144)
MILNE	John	Hangman, 1810. See Andrew Hosack. (167)
MILNE	Margaret	Daughter of and murdered along with George Milne (qv), 1797. (144)
MILNE	Thomas	Killed in Ross & Cromarty Rangers riot, 1802. (153)
MILNE	William	Murdered by James Wilson (qv), 1763. (60)
MITCHELL	Alex	Writer, Aberdeen. Juror in Northfield case, 1766. (68)
MITCHELL	Helen	Burnside, Keig. Poisoned 1821 by brother-in-law George Thom (qv), but recovered. (179)
MITCHELL	James	Burnside, Keig. Poisoned 1821 by brother-in-law George Thom (qv), but recovered. (179)
MITCHELL	Jean	Burnside, Keig. Wife of and poisoned by George Thom (qv) 1821 but recovered. (179)
MITCHELL	Robert	Tenant of farm in Mortlach. Outlawed 1774 for non-appearance on murder charge. (106)
MITCHELL	William	Burnside, Keig. Murdered 1821 by brother-in-law George Thom (qv). (179)
MOIR	(Dr.) Andrew	With other doctors built Anatomical School, St. Andrews Street. This was destroyed by mob in 1831. (218)
MOIR	Alexander	Minister of Free Church, St. Fergus. Witness 1854 in trial of Dr. William Smith (qv). (270)
MOIR	Christian	Deaf mute. Allegedly raped 1816 by Alexander Martin (qv) at Woodland. (198)
MOIR	John	Newtown of Northfield. Witness in Northfield case, 1766. (68)

MOIR	John	'Boy.' Killed in Ross & Cromarty Rangers riot, 1802. (153)
MOLLISON	John	Recruit in 73rd Regiment. Murdered 1778 by 2 Irish recruits at Castlebrae. (109)
MOODIE	David	'Countryman'. Helped to apprehend James Davidson (qv), 1748. (2)
MORISON	Alexander	Guestrow, Aberdeen. Murdered wife Agnes Yule, 1776. Hanged in Gallowgate. (107)
MORISON	James	Minister of Kinnell. Robbed of £25 by James Davidson (qv), 1747. (2)
MORISON	Theodore	of Bognie. 'Chancellor' of jury which convicted Alexander Cheyne (qv). Tried to persuade Cheyne to name associates and get commutation of sentence. (6)
MORRIS	Francis Enoch	German (?) Found not guilty of cursing Royal Family, 1753. (27)
MORRISON	William	Farm Servant. Outseats of Cullen, Gamrie. Believed to have murdered Elspet Imlach 1800 at Montcoffer but never taken. Outlawed. (145)
MORTIMER	Isobel	Banished 1758 for child murder. (53)
MUNRO	John (1)	Noted thief. See Peter Young. Hanged in 1787(?). (126)
MUNRO	John (2)	alias Stewart alias Brown alias Young. Johnshaven. Convicted 1788 of housebreaking etc. Whipped through streets and banished. Later convicted of housebreaking and executed, 1789. (134)
MUNRO	Mary	Servant aged 17 near Banff. Raped 1794 by William Turnbull (qv). (142)
MURDOCH	William	Jailer, Aberdeen Tolbooth up to 1747. (51)
MURISON	William	Blacksmith in Kirktown, St. Fergus. Witness 1854 in trial of Dr. William Smith (qv). (270)
MURRAY	Andrew	Pled guilty to mobbing and rioting, not guilty of fire-raising and assault, 1831. See Dr. Andrew Moir. 12 months' imprisonment. (218)

MURRAY	James	Servant to James Moseley, silk manufacturer. Killed in scuffle with Robert Brand (qv), 1766. (81)
MURRAY	Margaret	Murdered 1849 by husband James Burnett (qv) at Shelmanae, Tyrie. Name also of their daughter, a witness in the case. (248)
MURRAY	Margaret	Greenhill of Auchiries. Subject of 'stouthrief' 1823 at hands of William and Neil Macleod (qv). (195)
NESBIT	(Rev.) William	Minister of united parishes of Firth and Stenness in Orkney. Convicted 1766 of adultery with a Mrs. Agnew. Banished for life. (40)
NICOL	Janet	Charged 1790 with perjury at trial of John Munro (qv). (135)
OGILVIE	John	Jesuit. Executed 1750 for declining jurisdiction of Court to compel him to answer certain questions. (21)
PARK	James	Shopman to Alex M'Leod, merchant, St. Fergus. Witness 1854 in trial of Dr. William Smith (qv). (270)
PATERSON	Alexander	Sailor. Charged along with Alex Wiseman with murder of fortune-teller in Gardenstown 1768 but escaped and outlawed. (82)
PATERSON	James	Huckster in Aberdeen. Sentenced to be hanged for housebreaking and theft, but committed suicide in his cell, 1758. (53)
PAUL	John	Sentenced to death 1787 for sheep-stealing. See Peter Young. (126)
PETRIE	Robert	Auchmadies. Juryman in Northfield case, 1766. (68)
PHILLIP	William	Herdsman, Southside, St. Fergus. Witness 1854 in trial of Dr. William Smith (qv). (270)
PHILP	Alexander	Butcher. Episcopalian. Charged along with Alex Macdonald with murder of Robert Esson of Woolmanhill and theft from one Wilkie, a carrier. Found guilty and executed, 1749. (16)

PHILP	Anne		Stonehaven. Wife of Henry Buchanan, Officer of Excise. Convicted of murder of her child, 1749. Sentenced to be hanged but later pardoned. (15)
PHILP	'Doctor' George		Huntly. Convicted of procuring abortion 1771 and transported to plantations. (89)
PHILP	William		Farmer at Stodfield of Skelmuir. Convicted of horse-stealing. Perpetual banishment, 1769. (84)
PHREN	Christian		Farm servant. Murdered her illegitimate child. Executed Gallowhills, 24 November 1752. (24)
PIRIE	Patrick		Malhereust, Alva. Murdered 1795 allegedly by Anne Inglis (qv). (142)
PIRRIE	James		Farmer, St. Fergus. Witness 1854 in trial of Dr. William Smith (qv). (270)
POTTS	William		Soldier in Lord Hopetoun's Fencibles. Charged with aiding and abetting William Turnbull (qv) 1794, but pardoned on condition entered King's service. (142)
PRIDE	Alexander		Tailor in Edinburgh. Child George stolen 1783 by Margaret Irvine (qv). (115)
PRIDE	George		Child of Alexander Pride, Edinburgh. Stolen 1783 by Margaret Irvine (qv). (115)
RATE	Sarah Sophia		Aged 14 or 15. Sentenced 1862 to 9 months' imprisonment for concealment of pregnancy. (293)
RAY	Elizabeth		Huntly. Said to have asked 'Dr' George Philp (qv) to arrange abortion for her, 1770. (89)
REID	Elspet		Banffshire. Convicted 11 June 1784 of theft and housebreaking. Execution deferred on plea she was pregnant, but hanged 14 January 1785 - presumably after giving birth. (113)
REID	Helen		Tried and condemned 1816 for murder of husband James in Keith. Commuted to perpetual banishment. (170)

REID	James	Vintner and mail contractor in Keith. Murdered 1816 by wife Helen (qv). (170)
REID	Janet	Fyvie. Charged 1817 with murder of infant of Isabel Milne, fellow-servant. Not proven. (171)
RICHARDSON	?	'The rural police at Printfield'. Witness in case of George Christie (qv), 1852. (264)
RITCHIE	James (1)	Aged under 20. Convicted of theft and hanged. Mid 19th Century? (106)
RITCHIE	James (2)	Murdered at Mill of Kinairdy, 1782, by William Ross (qv). (110)
RITCHIE	James (3)	Aged 17 in 1818. Parish of Gamrie. Stole 30 sheep from parks of Gordon Castle. Executed despite efforts of many for pardon. (171)
RITCHIE	William	'A lad from Kildrummy'. Charged 1844 with murder of father. Pled guilty to culpable homicide. 15 years' transportation. (239)
ROBB	Alexander	Banff. Stealing meal from ship at Banff. Sentenced to be whipped and banished to plantations but released by mob, 1766. (66)
ROBB	James	Labourer in slate quarry, aged 22 when convicted 1849 of rape and murder of Mary Smith, Redhill, Auchterless. Hanged by 'Calcraft, the celebrated executioner....from London'. (256)
ROBERTSON	Alexander	Agent in Peterhead for Scottish Mutual Insurance Co. Witness 1854 in trial of Dr. William Smith (qv). (270)
ROBERTSON	(Rev.) James	St. Fergus. Witness 1854 in trial of Dr. William Smith (qv). (270)
ROBERTSON	John	Banff. Convicted 1817 of shopbreaking and transported for life. (171)
RODGER or ROGER	James	House carpenter, Aberdeen. Cheques forged 1878 by Robert Mackenzie (qv). (313)

ROSENBERG	Harris		Charged along with wife Alethia Barnett with arson at shop in Union Street, 1842. Transportation for life. (235)
ROSS	Barbara		Sunnybank near Kittybrewster Toll-bar. Engaged in 'cowfeeding' etc. Murdered 1852 with grandson by George Christie (qv). (264)
ROSS	Christian		Vagrant suspected of thieving, 1761. (56)
ROSS	Isobel		Balvach. Allegedly raped by John Thomson and John Watt, 1754. (50)
ROSS	John		Rifleman. Killed in Ross & Cromarty Rangers riot, 1802. (153)
ROSS	William		Whitemair, Marnoch. Outlawed 1782 for non-appearance on charge of murdering James Ritchie (2). (110)
RUNCEY	Charles		Merchant. Witness 1832 in case of Alex Milne (qv). (227)
SANGSTER	James		Watchman in Gallowgate. Nicknamed 'Satan'. Sold wife's body to anatomists. Early 19th Century. (56)
SCOTCHIE	Thomas		Drummer to puppet show. Guilty of assaulting Barbara Wilson in Bomakettle with intent to ravish, 1749. Sentenced to be publicly whipped through Aberdeen. (18)
SCOTT	James		Piper, Ellon. Charged 1756 but released along with Alex Lorimer (qv). (52)
SHAND	Isabella		Pled guilty to culpable homicide of her child 1864 and sentenced to 4 years' penal servitude. (293)
SHARPE	George		Pled guilty to mobbing and rioting, not guilty of fire-raising and assault, 1831. See Dr. Andrew Moir. 12 months' imprisonment. (218)
SIEVEWRIGHT	Charles		Boatman at Boat-of-Haughead. Said to have murdered James Downie 1768, but escaped. (84)

SIM	Margaret	alias Lucky Walker. Wife of John Walker. Charged 1786 with keeping a house of bad fame etc. Sentenced to stand in pillory, be drummed through streets, and banished the city. (120)
SIMPSON	Agnes	Charged 1786 and 1796 with murder of child but found insane. Perpetual confinement in Banff jail. (121)
SIMPSON	George	Gravedigger, Strichen. Witness 1849 in case of James Burnett (qv). (248)
SIMPSON	James	A 'boy' in 1849 when sentenced to 7 years' transportation for theft. (262)
SIMPSON	John	'The Black Drummer', 29th Regt. Murdered 1807 allegedly by Donald Macallum, Daniel Macpherson and James Graham (qv). (162)
SKINNNER	Peter	Convicted 1804 for theft from body of Francis Mollison. Pilloried, imprisoned, banished for 7 years', whipped on return. Witness 1807 in case of John Simpson. (162)
SLESSOR or MACDONALD	Elizabeth	Witness 1849 in case of James Burnett (qv). (248)
SLESSOR	Mary	St. Fergus. About to be married 1853 to William M'Donald (qv) when he was murdered. (270)
SMALL	(Ensign) James	General Guise's Regiment. Witness in case of murder of Sgt. Davis. (41)
SMITH	Helen	Wife of John Dun. Associate of James Davidson (qv). (2)
SMITH	James	Saddler. Ex-Convener of Trades. Pursued for criminal slander by Ex-Provost Alexander Livingstone (qv), whom he had alleged to be responsible for rise in cost of meal. Court found for Livingstone. Smith asked pardon in court and was dismissed, 1753. (33)
SMITH	James Jnr.	Cartwright in Kirktown, St. Fergus. Witness in trial of Dr. William Smith (qv), 1854. (270)
SMITH	Jane	Huntly. Found not guilty 1860 of concealment of pregnancy. (293)

SMITH	Janet		Glass. Natural daughter of Isobel Macdonald, wife of Alex Christie (qv). Outlawed for non-appearance on charge of incest and adultery with latter. (106)
SMITH	John		Guilty of horse-stealing 1749, and executed 2nd June. (9)
SMITH	Mary		Aged 63 in 1849 when raped and murdered by James Robb (qv). (256)
SMITH	William		Sheriff Officer, Peterhead. Witness 1854 in trial of Dr. William Smith (qv). (270)
SMITH	(Dr.) William		Medical practitioner in St. Fergus. Wife's m.s. Lawrence. Tried 1854 for murder of William M'Donald, but charge found 'not proven'. (270)
SMOLLET	Arthur		Charged 1815 with rioting etc. at house of Mgt. Dick (qv). 12 months' confinement in Bridewell. (168)
SORRIE	Janet m.s. Anderson		or wife of George Sorrie, Waukmill of Wardhouse. Shopbreaking, 1771. Imprisoned, then 'placed in the pillory'. (90)
SOUPER	Patrick		Achlounnies. Juryman in Northfield case, 1766. (68)
SOUTER	William		Aged 20. Son of Lord Halkerston's ground officer. Sentenced to hang 1774 for theft of cattle, but this commuted to banishment to plantations for life. (106)
SPENCE	Christian		Wife of John Gray, Pitmedden, Dyce. Along with James Gray charged with fire-raising. After period of imprisonment, had to find caution for good behaviour for 3 years. 1770. (88)
STABLES	Thomas		Soldier. Convicted 1751 of shooting William Gow, Auchenrach, Cabrach, whom he had challenged for wearing tartan. Sentenced to death but later given free pardon. (23)

STEPHEN	George	Woodmerchant, Port-Elphinstone, aged 62. Convicted of murder in 1864 of Ann Forbes (qv). Sentenced to hang but confined to asylum for life. (295)
STEVEN	Jean	Banished 1755 or '56 for child-murder. (52)
STEVENSON	Janet	Witness 1790 in case of James Henderson and Eliz. Stewart (qv). (136)
STEWART	Ann	Convicted 1835 of culpable homicide of James Thow, Fettercairn. 6 months' imprisonment. (225)
STEWART	Charles	Bricklaw, New Deer. Outlawed 1789 for non-appearance on charge of housebreaking at Cairnbulg. See also John Munro and James Stewart. (135)
STEWART	Duncan	Witness 1821 in case of Robt. Mackintosh. (187)
STEWART	Elizabeth	Wife of James Henderson. Charged along with him with murder of Alex Gillespie, 1790. Not proven. (136)
STEWART	James	Servant to John Copland. Murdered by John Wattie (qv), 1754. (55)
STEWART	James	Overhill of Foveran. Not guilty 1789 of housebreaking at Cairnbulg. See also John Munro and Charles Stewart. Banished the country 1790. (135)
STEWART	John	See John Munro (2).
STEWART	John	Tenant in Abergairn. Murdered 1747 by Malcolm Macgregor (qv). (100)
STEWART	John	Tenant of Wester Clashmarloch, Aberdour. Guilty of culpable homicide of Francis Middleton, 1838. (229)
STEWART	(Major) Ludovic	JP at Banff. Witness in case of assault on Francis Middleton by John Stewart, 1838. (229)
STEWART or WISEMAN	Margaret	Theft. Sentenced 1849 to 7 years' transportation. (255)

STEWART	Martha	Died 1785 as result of abortion allegedly procured by Robt. Joyner and Robt. Dalrymple (qv). (118)
STEWART	Thomas	'Caird' from Kirriemuir. Spoonmaker. Convicted of murder of David Thomson at market-stance in Stonehaven 1770 while resisting arrest. Hanged. (87)
STILL	William	Butcher. Confined in Strathbogie for sheep-stealing. Hanged self by garters before taken to Aberdeen for trial, 1751. (23)
STRACHAN	Elspet	Convicted 1753 along with husband John Walker of keeping lewd and disorderly house. Banished the city. (40)
STRACHAN	George	Found guilty of theft from farmer at Craigievar market, 1860. 7 years' penal servitude. (292)
STRACHAN	James	Mill of Kincardine. Peter Young (qv) and others surprised in attempt to rob his house, 1787. (126)
STRACHAN	John	Coffin-maker. Witness in Northfield case, 1766. (68)
STUART	Angus	'Very respectable'. Charged 1858 along with James Stuart with culpable homicide or assault. Pled guilty to latter. 3 months' imprisonment. (290)
STUART	James	'Very respectable'. Charged 1858 along with Angus Stuart with culpable homicide or assault. Pled guilty to latter. 3 months' imprisonment. (290)
SUTHERLAND	(Sgt.) Alexander	Ross & Cromarty Rangers. Charged with murder of John Ross in 1802 riot. Not proven. (153)
SUTHERLAND	Daniel	Stonehaven. Associate of Thomas Stewart (qv), 1770. (87)
TAWSE or BUCHAN	Catherine	Assistant in shop of William Howe, spirit-dealer, Adelphi Lane. Assaulted by husband William (qv), 1860. (292)

TAWSE	William	Tailor. Found guilty 1860 of throwing vitriol at wife Catherine in shop in Adelphi Lane. 5 years' penal servitude. (292)
TAYLOR	Agnes	alias Snippy Associate of John Gun (qv). (37)
TAYLOR	Barbara	Pled guilty 1864 to child-murder and sentenced to 10 years' penal servitude. (293)
TAYLOR	John	Whitefisher in Stonehaven. Charged 1753 with adultery with Helen King (qv). Fled and outlawed. (39)
TAYLOR	William	Darfash. Servant. Witness in Northfield case, 1766. (68)
TAYLOR	William	Student of medicine. Witness 1838 to assault by John Stewart on Francis Middleton (qv). (229)
TERIG	Duncan	See Duncan Clerk.
THOM	George	Farmer, Harthill, Newmills. Convicted of murder of brother-in-law William Mitchell, 1821. Hanged. Also alleged murderer of Thomas Gill, 1817. (179)
THOMPSON	Hugh	alias William Cameron. 'Expert burglar from the south country' (Edinburgh?). Convicted 1844 or '48 of housebreaking. 14 years' transportation. (243)
THOMPSON	William	Found guilty of theft despite plea of insanity. 7 years' transportation. (256)
THOMSON	Alexander	Jailer at Aberdeen Tolbooth 1747, dismissed by Council for allowing prisoners to escape. (51)
THOMSON	David	Slater in Stonehaven. Killed 1770 in process of helping constable to arrest Thomas Stewart (qv). (87)
THOMSON or GRAY	Janet	Tinker, aged 35 in 1849 when charged along with William Clark (qv) with murder of latter's wife. Not proven. (259)

THOMSON	John		Strila in parish of Cluny. Charged 1754 along with John Watt with rape of Isobel Ross. Not proven. (50)
THOW	James		Crofter, Moss-side of Arnhall, Fettercairn. Died after assault by Ann Stewart (qv), 1835. (225)
TROUP	William		Sentenced 1849 to 7 years' transportation for theft. (255)
TURNBULL	William		Soldier in Lord Hopetoun's Fencibles. Charged 1794 with rape. Found guilty, sentenced to death, but pardoned on condition entered King's service. (142)
WAST	William		Seaman. Seatown of Auchmedden. Hanged at Gallowhills 1752 for murder of wife. (25)
WALKER	James		Apprentice to Mr. Mitchell, gunsmith, Peterhead. Witness 1854 in trial of Dr. William Smith (qv). (270)
WALKER	John		Barber. Convicted 1753 along with wife Elspet Strachan of keeping lewd and disorderly house. Banished the city. (40)
WALKER	John		Husband of Margaret Sim (qv). (120)
WALKER	Lucky		Alias Margaret SIM (qv). (120)
WATSON	George		Cooper, Gallowgate. Charged 1819 with falsely accusing John Hamilton of housebreaking. Transported for 14 years. (176)
WATT	Helen		Charged 1766 along with son William Keith with murder of husband Alexander Keith of Northfield. Condemned to death but later pardoned. (68)
WATT	Jane		Aged 24 when sentenced to 9 months' imprisonment for concealment of pregnancy in 1862. (293)
WATT	Jean		Charged with theft of cloak which she sold to Margaret Sim (qv). Banished the city, 1786. (120)

WATT	James		alias Duncan. 'Expert burglar from the south country' (Edinburgh?). Convicted 1844 or '48 of housebreaking. Sentenced to 10 years' transportation. (243)
WATT	Janet		Servant. Witness in Northfield case, 1766. (68)
WATT	John		Quarrier of Lochead near Aberdeen. Charged 1754 along with John Thomson with rape of Isobel Ross. Not proven. (50)
WATTIE	John		Farmer, parish of Towie. Charged 1759 with 1754 murder of boy, James Stewart. Transported to Virginia. (55)
WEBSTER	William		Ex-soldier, vagrant. Banished the city for operating wheel-of-fortune. Later charged with theft and executed 1787 in market place. (121)
WEMYSS	Henry		Sentenced 1849 to 7 years' transportation for theft. (256)
WEMYSS	William		Craighall. Juryman in Northfield case, 1766. (68)
WHITECROSS or MARSHALL	Helen		Sentenced 1849 to 12 months' imprisonment for uttering counterfeit coins. (255)
WILLIAMSON	John		Chainmaker. Killed 1841 by William Bruce (qv). (233)
WILLIAMSON	William		son of James Williamson, keeper of public-house at Cairnhill on road to Stonehaven. Involved along with father and brother Peter in affray in which Charles Burnett killed, and Lieut. Farquharson injured. William charged with murder but acquitted, 1769. (85)
WILSON	Barbara		Bomakettle. Assaulted by Thomas Scotchie (qv), 1749. (18)
WILSON	James		Beheaded, Edinburgh, 1649 for incest commited 35 years before with wife's daughter. (103)
WILSON	James		Parkburn, Leslie. Outlawed 1763 for non-appearance on charge of murdering William Milne. (59)

WILSON	James		Minister at Gamrie. Witness in Northfield case, 1766. (68)
WILSON	Jean		Wife of Peter Young (qv). Sentence of death for shopbreaking deferred 1787 because of pregnancy. Escaped, retaken, and in 1791 shipped to London for transportation to New South Wales. (124)
WILSON	William		Mill of Macterry, parish of Fyvie. Associate of Alex Cheyne (qv). Guilty of robbery. Sentenced to be hung but escaped, 1749. (8)
WISEMAN	Alexander		Sailor. Charged along with Alex Paterson with murder of fortune-teller in Gardenstown 1768, but escaped and outlawed. (82)
WISEMAN	Margaret		See Margaret Stewart.
WRIGHT	Isobel		Echt. Raped by Alexander Irvine (qv), 1754. (51)
WRIGHT	Rachel		Charged 1808 in Glasgow with theft of child, Flora Amos. Banished for life. (117)
YOUNG	John		See John Munro. (2)
YOUNG	John		Brother of Peter (qv). Convicted 1801 of murder of Hugh Graham and executed. (150)
YOUNG	Melitta or Amelia or Muletta		'Caird' in troop of vagrants. Banished the county, 1772. (124)
YOUNG	Peter or Patrick		'Caird'. Native of Deeside. Noted and resourceful thief, said to have escaped from every jail in Scotland. Convicted 1787 of shopbreaking in Portsoy, but broke jail and released all prisoners. Eventually executed aged 23 in 1788 at Edinburgh Tolbooth. (124)
YOUNG	Silvester		'Caird' in troop of vagrants. Banished the county, 1772. (124)
YULE	Agnes		Murdered 1776 by husband Alex Morison, Guestrow. (107)